Somatic Therapy For Kids

How Parents, Therapists, and Teachers Can Help Children Heal Anxiety, Trauma, and Stress Through Body Awareness and Connection

ROWAN MASON

Copyright © **2025 by Rowan Mason**

All rights reserved. This book may not be copied, stored, or shared in any format whether electronic, mechanical, photocopied, recorded, or otherwise without the prior written consent of the author, except for short excerpts used in reviews or scholarly articles.

Disclaimer

This book is for educational purposes and does not provide medical, psychological, or emergency advice. It is not a substitute for diagnosis, personalized treatment, or therapy. Always consult a licensed health professional about a child's specific needs. Do not begin any new intervention that feels unsafe to the child. If you believe a child is in danger, or there is risk of harm to self or others, call local emergency services or a crisis line immediately. School-based professionals must follow their jurisdiction's reporting and consent requirements.

Dedication

To the children
whose bodies hold stories too big for words,
and whose courage to heal teaches us what safety
truly means.

To the parents, therapists, and teachers
who stay, breathe, and believe even when it's hard.
Your presence is the medicine.

And to every child within us
still learning to come home to the body,
may this work be a soft place to land.

Rowan Mason

Table of Contents

Introduction..6
When Words Aren't Enough...6
Chapter 1..13
The Body as the Storyteller.. 13
Chapter 2..23
Safety First: The Nervous System in Action................ 23
Chapter 3..36
Co-Regulation: Calming Through Connection..............36
Chapter 4..49
Somatic Awareness: Teaching Kids to Notice Their Bodies.. 49
Chapter 5..63
Movement as Medicine..63
Chapter 6..77
Touch, Breath, and Grounding: Tools for Emotional Safety.. 77
Chapter 7..91
Emotional Literacy: Helping Children Name and Express Feelings.. 91
Chapter 8..104
Play, Creativity, and Healing Through Imagination.... 104
Chapter 9..117
The Role of Parents and Caregivers: Becoming the Child's Safe Base... 117
Chapter 10..129

Integrating Somatic Practice at Home and School...... 129
Conclusion... 142
Coming Home to the Body... 142

Introduction

When Words Aren't Enough

The Child Who Couldn't Explain

The first time I met Ella, she was six years old and furious.

She'd been sent to therapy because she'd started hitting other children at school and hiding under her desk when teachers approached. Her parents described her as "difficult" and "unpredictable." When I sat down across from her, she didn't speak. She crossed her arms, scowled, and stared at the floor.

Ten minutes passed in silence. Then, as I reached to roll a soft therapy ball toward her, she kicked it hard against the wall. It wasn't defiance, it was desperation. Her little body was saying what her words couldn't: *I'm scared, I'm angry, I don't know what to do with all this energy inside me.*

That moment changed everything I knew about helping children.

Because when words fail, the body doesn't.

Why Words Fall Short

We often ask children to *"use their words."* We say it with good intentions, believing that if they can name a feeling, they can control it. But the truth is, under stress, a child's brain goes offline. The body takes over.

When fear or frustration hits, blood flow moves away from the parts of the brain that handle language and reasoning. What's left is movement, tone, breathing, posture the body's ancient vocabulary of survival. A clenched jaw, restless legs, or rigid shoulders aren't misbehavior. They're messages. They're the nervous system's way of saying, *I don't feel safe right now.*

Somatic therapy teaches us to listen to that language. It reminds us that the body isn't the problem; it's the storyteller. The child who can't talk about fear might stomp it out, spin it out, or collapse under its weight. If we learn to listen to the body first, words often follow naturally, not forced, but freed.

The Hidden World Beneath Behavior

Think about the last time a child's reaction felt "too big." The tantrum over a broken crayon. The panic at a loud noise. The sudden silence when a stranger entered the room.

It's easy to focus on what we see: yelling, crying, withdrawing. But underneath, the body is doing something brilliant trying to protect itself. That's what nervous systems do. They choose survival over social grace every time.

When we understand that, the story changes. We stop asking, *"What's wrong with this child?"* and start asking, *"What's happening in this child's body?"* That shift is where healing begins.

Somatic therapy doesn't punish reactions. It meets them with curiosity. It says: *Your body is telling the truth. Let's help it feel safe enough to rest.*

Relearning to Listen

Every behavior no matter how chaotic or confusing is communication.

The child who lashes out isn't trying to hurt; they're trying to discharge unbearable energy. The one who shuts down isn't rejecting you; they're retreating to survive. Even joy, silliness, and restlessness are messages from the body about how energy moves and settles.

When we begin to see behavior through this lens, everything softens. Our job changes from *discipline* to *translation*. Instead of asking for better behavior, we start listening for what the body is saying underneath the noise.

And when a child feels understood at that level, trust begins to grow not just between you and them, but inside their own body.

The Story This Book Will Tell

Somatic Therapy for Kids is not a parenting manual or a clinical textbook. It's a bridge between science and intuition, between body and mind, between adult and child.

You'll learn:

- How the nervous system shapes behavior and emotion.

- How to recognize the body's signals of stress and safety.

- How to use movement, touch, and sensory awareness to restore calm.

- How your own body becomes the model for a child's regulation.

- How to turn everyday moments into healing opportunities.

Each chapter will blend gentle science with real-world examples, guiding you to practice these concepts in small, manageable steps.

You'll find reflection questions, somatic exercises, and stories from families who've learned to see and soothe their children differently.

A Different Kind of Hope

This isn't about fixing children. It's about freeing them.

Children don't need to be perfect; they need to feel safe. And they learn that safety through the way we *see*, *listen*, and *move with* them. Somatic therapy reminds us that emotional healing doesn't live in words alone, it lives in the rhythm of breath, the warmth of presence, the quiet heartbeat that says: *You are safe. You are home.*

So before you turn the page, take a breath.
Notice your shoulders, your chest, the ground beneath your feet.
You've already begun the work. Because somatic healing starts not with doing, but with noticing not with instruction, but with connection.

Chapter 1

The Body as the Storyteller

The Child Who Spoke Without Words

When eight-year-old Milo first came to therapy, his parents described him as "angry all the time." He refused to go to school, slammed doors, and sometimes hid in his closet for hours. He rarely spoke about how he felt. When I asked what made him angry, he shrugged. But his body told the story his mouth could not.

His shoulders were pulled tight toward his ears. His jaw clenched every time his mother raised her voice. His legs bounced under the chair like he was ready to run. When I asked him to take a deep breath, he held it. Not out of defiance or out of habit. His body had learned that stillness could be unsafe.

Over time, Milo didn't need to tell me his story in words. His posture, his breathing, his tension spoke volumes. And slowly, as we worked through play and movement, his body began to soften. His voice followed.

This is where every story in somatic therapy begins not in the mind, but in the body.

Why the Body Speaks First

From the moment we're born, our bodies keep track of every experience. Long before children can talk, their nervous systems collect information about the world: what feels safe, what feels threatening, what brings comfort, what brings pain.

When something frightening or overwhelming happens, the body reacts before the brain has time to make sense of it. The heart races, muscles tense, breathing changes. These reactions are automatic, the body's way of protecting itself. For many children, especially those who've faced early stress or trauma, these patterns can become stuck.

Later, when a teacher says something sharp or a friend takes a toy, the body remembers that earlier threat. It reacts again not to the moment, but to the echo of what came before. That's why a small trigger can lead to a big reaction. The body isn't overreacting; it's remembering.

In this way, behavior is not random. It's the nervous system's best attempt to stay safe. When we understand that, we can meet children with compassion instead of judgment.

Behavior as Body Language

When a child screams, runs, or shuts down, we often ask, "Why are you acting like this?" But what if we asked instead, "What is your body trying to say right now?"

A child's movements, expressions, and tension patterns are their first language. The body says what the mouth cannot:

- The child who fidgets constantly may not be inattentive; they may be trying to discharge nervous energy.

- The one who freezes during conflict may not be ignoring you; they may be in a shutdown state, their body conserving energy to survive.

- The one who talks nonstop or makes jokes in serious moments may be using movement and sound to stay connected when stillness feels dangerous.

These patterns aren't manipulative. They're protective. And when adults begin to see them that way, everything changes.

The Science of Somatic Memory

Neuroscience confirms what therapists have witnessed for decades: the body stores emotional memory. Dr. Bessel van der Kolk, in *The Body Keeps the Score*, explains that when the brain cannot process an experience through language or logic, it records it through sensation tightness in the chest, a knot in the stomach, a flinch at a raised voice.

For children, this process is amplified. Their prefrontal cortex, the part of the brain responsible for reasoning and self-regulation, is still developing. Meanwhile, their limbic system and brainstem, the emotional and survival centers dominate their responses.

This means that under stress, a child's body reacts *first* and thinks *later*. Their emotional world is experienced through the senses: sound, touch, sight, and movement.

That's why somatic therapy works so well for children. It honors their native language, the body's language and helps them learn how to listen, understand, and respond from the inside out.

Reading the Body with Compassion

When adults learn to read body language accurately, they stop taking behavior personally. They begin to recognize the subtle cues that show when a child is nearing overwhelm a change in breathing, a shift in tone, a look of wide-eyed alertness.

Instead of saying, "Stop fidgeting," they might say, "I notice your legs are moving a lot. Do you feel restless?"

Instead of "Use your words," they might say, "Your shoulders look tight. Let's take a breath together."

This small change from correction to observation builds trust. It tells the child, "I see you," not "You're wrong."

The adult becomes a translator for the body's messages, helping the child make sense of what's happening inside. Over time, this awareness helps children find their own words, not through force, but through safety.

How the Body Holds Both Pain and Strength

Every child's body carries a story not just of stress, but of survival. The same nervous system that tenses in fear also allows for laughter, play, and creativity. The same muscles that brace for danger can dance, climb, and explore.

Somatic therapy isn't about erasing tension. It's about helping the body rediscover flexibility, the ability to move between tension and ease, alertness and rest. This is what regulation really means: not constant calm, but the ability to return to balance after disruption.

When children learn that their bodies are not enemies but allies, they begin to trust themselves. They discover that big feelings aren't dangerous, just messages to be understood.

And when adults model this when they meet emotion with steady breath and grounded presence children learn safety not as a concept, but as a felt experience.

A New Kind of Listening

Listening to the body requires slowing down. It means pausing before reacting, noticing before judging. In our fast-paced world, that's not easy. But it's the foundation of connection.

Next time a child screams or withdraws, take a breath and look deeper.

Ask yourself:

- What might their body be protecting them from right now?

- What signal of safety do they need a softer tone, more space, a steady presence?

When you begin to see beyond behavior, you'll realize something profound: every child is already communicating. We just need to learn their dialect.

The Beginning of Healing

Milo, the boy who once hid in his closet, eventually stopped needing to hide. Not because I taught him to "behave," but because his body learned what safety felt like. Through play, rhythm, and gentle movement, he discovered that he could release energy without fear.

His shoulders dropped. His breathing deepened. He laughed more often. And slowly, words returned. When he finally said, "Sometimes my body gets too full," I knew he understood. His body had spoken all along; it just needed someone to listen.

Reflection for the Reader

Take a quiet moment. Think of a time when your child or student's behavior confused or frustrated you.

What might their body have been saying through that moment?

Notice how your own body feels as you recall it, the tightening in your chest, the warmth in your hands, the quickened breath.

That awareness is the first step toward connection.

Because before we can listen to a child's body, we must first learn to listen to our own.

Chapter 2

Safety First: The Nervous System in Action

The Day Safety Disappeared

In the therapy room, nine-year-old Jaden sat frozen in his chair. He wasn't crying. He wasn't fidgeting. He was completely still. His teacher had described him as "shutting down" when things got hard especially when someone raised their voice.

When I gently asked him what happens at school when the teacher gets upset, his eyes flicked toward the door, then back to the floor. No answer. His small hands gripped the seat so tightly his knuckles turned white. I could see it: his body was no longer here in the room. His nervous system had already chosen safety by disappearing inside itself.

Moments like this are common. Children don't *decide* to freeze, yell, or hide; their bodies do it for them. And until we understand that these reactions are biological, not behavioral, we'll keep trying to reason with a body that isn't listening.

The Body's Alarm System

Every human body comes equipped with a built-in alarm, the autonomic nervous system. It's the invisible network that controls heartbeat, breathing, digestion, and countless reflexes. Its job is simple: keep you alive.

When a child perceives danger, even something as small as a sharp tone or a disappointed glance, their nervous system asks one question: *Am I safe?* If the answer feels like "no," the body prepares for survival. Heart rate rises, muscles tighten, pupils widen. It's not rebellion, it's protection.

This system has three main states:

1. **Safe and Connected (Ventral Vagal State)** — The body feels calm. Breathing is steady. The child is open to learning, playing, and relating.

2. **Mobilized (Sympathetic State)** — The body senses threat. Energy floods in. The child may become restless, angry, impulsive, or defensive.

3. **Shut Down (Dorsal Vagal State)** — When escape seems impossible, the body collapses inward. The child may become numb, silent, or "zoned out."

Every behavior we see in children, every tantrum, withdrawal, or meltdown fits somewhere along this ladder.

Why Safety Comes Before Reason

Parents often try to talk a child out of a meltdown: *"Calm down." "You're fine." "Use your words."* But reasoning only works when the child's body feels safe.

The part of the brain that handles logic the prefrontal cortex goes offline when the nervous system senses danger. It's not a lack of willpower. It's biology. The thinking brain can't function when the survival brain has taken the wheel.

That's why the calmest thing you can do in those moments isn't to talk, it's to *be*.
Your tone, your breath, your body posture these speak louder than words. A slow exhale or a soft expression can tell a child's nervous system: *You're safe now. You can come back.*

Once safety returns, reason follows naturally. Until then, connection is the only bridge to logic.

The Many Faces of Unsafety

Children rarely say, "I feel unsafe." Instead, their bodies announce it for them.

A child in a **mobilized state** might shout, throw things, run, or talk nonstop. They look "wild" because their system is flooded with energy and adrenaline. They're trying to move the danger out.

A child in a **shutdown state** looks the opposite quiet, detached, unreachable. They might stare blankly, whisper, or avoid eye contact. They're not ignoring you; they've simply gone into energy conservation mode.

And here's the most important thing: both are protective responses. Both are attempts to survive. When we understand that, our question shifts from "How do I stop this?" to "How do I help this body feel safe again?"

Tiny Triggers, Big Reactions

For adults, a loud voice or a sudden change might be mildly annoying. For a child whose nervous system is sensitive or shaped by early stress, it can feel like danger.

Maybe their body remembers a time when yelling led to pain. Or when change meant loss. Even if they can't recall those moments consciously, their body does. The nervous system has no sense of time, it responds as though the old threat is happening again right now.

That's why safety is never just about what's *true, it's* about what feels true.

A calm environment, consistent routine, and gentle tone can all tell a child's body: *The danger has passed.*

How Adults Signal Safety

Children learn safety through the people around them. Every look, tone, and gesture we use becomes a cue their nervous system reads.

You've probably noticed this in your own life: one person's voice can make you tense, another's can instantly calm you. It's the same for children, only magnified.

Here's what signals safety to a child's body:

- A relaxed face and steady eye contact

- A warm tone of voice, even when setting limits

- Slow, rhythmic movements (like rocking, breathing, or swaying)

- Predictable patterns routines that tell the nervous system what's coming next

Safety doesn't mean perfection. It means consistency. A calm adult is not one who never gets upset, but one who can come back to center quickly. That ability to regulate and repair teaches the child's body that connection is reliable.

The Repair After Disconnection

No adult stays regulated all the time. We lose patience, raise our voices, or withdraw. What matters is what happens next.

When an adult says, "I got too loud earlier. I'm sorry if that scared you. I'm calm now, and you're safe," they do something remarkable: they model repair.

In that moment, the child's nervous system learns that safety can return even after disconnection. It's not the absence of rupture that heals, it's the presence of repair.

Somatic therapy focuses on this dance between rupture and repair. The body learns safety through repetition: "Even when things get hard, we find our way back."

Case Reflection: Jaden's Return to Safety

With Jaden, I didn't start with questions. I started with rhythm. We rolled a soft ball back and forth in silence. I matched his breathing shallow at first, then gradually slower. His shoulders began to drop. His eyes lifted from the floor.

After a few minutes, he whispered, "Sometimes I feel like I disappear."

I nodded and said quietly, "Your body helps you disappear when it doesn't feel safe. But we can teach them that it's okay to stay."

Over the next few sessions, we practiced tiny grounding movements: pressing feet into the floor, stretching arms out wide, noticing the sound of his own breath. Each time, his body found a little more safety, and with it came more words, more connection.

Safety didn't arrive all at once. It grew in small, steady moments of presence.

How Safety Shapes Everything

A safe nervous system is the soil where learning, empathy, and creativity grow. Without it, the mind stays in survival mode, constantly scanning for threat instead of absorbing new experiences.

This is why some children struggle to focus, follow directions, or sit still. It's not disobedience, it's biology. Their bodies are too busy managing danger signals to care about math problems or manners.

Once their nervous system feels safe, everything else blooms: curiosity, playfulness, humor, compassion. Safety isn't a luxury; it's the foundation for every kind of growth.

Your Own Nervous System Matters Too

Children borrow regulation from adults, but adults have nervous systems of their own. A parent who's exhausted, anxious, or rushed will unconsciously signal that energy to the child.

Before helping a child calm down, pause and check in with your own body:
Are your shoulders tight? Is your breath shallow? Is your voice clipped?
Take one slow breath. Feel your feet on the ground. The moment you calm your body, you become the child's safety signal.

Regulation is contagious both ways. The more you practice it, the more your child will, too.

From Survival to Connection

Think of the nervous system as a ladder. At the top is safety, the space where curiosity, laughter, and empathy live. In the middle is mobilization alert and ready to act. At the bottom is shutdown quiet, still, disconnected.

Somatic therapy helps children climb back up this ladder, step by step, through body awareness and connection. It's not about teaching them to avoid strong feelings, but about showing them how to move through those states safely.

When a child learns that they can feel fear and still come back to calm, their body begins to trust the world again. That's the heart of emotional resilience.

Reflection for the Reader

Think of a moment when a child's reaction seemed "too much."

What might their nervous system have been trying to do fight, flee, or freeze?

Now think of how your own body responded in that moment. Did you tense, raise your voice, or withdraw?

Take a deep breath. Imagine approaching that same moment again, but this time as a signal of safety, steady voice, soft eyes, grounded posture.

How might that change the outcome for both of you?

Chapter 3

Co-Regulation: Calming Through Connection

The Power of Presence

Five-year-old Ava stormed into the playroom and slammed the door so hard that the window rattled. Her mother followed, flustered and apologetic. Ava refused to meet my eyes. She stood rigid, fists balled, breathing fast.

I didn't ask her to calm down. I didn't tell her to stop. I simply sat on the rug, exhaled slowly, and began stacking wooden blocks in a gentle rhythm one, two, three. Within a minute, her breathing slowed to match mine. She glanced over, curious. The storm was passing.

That moment had nothing to do with words or discipline. It was a co-regulation of two nervous systems finding rhythm together.

What Co-Regulation Really Is

Co-regulation is the biological process by which a child borrows an adult's calm. It's the nervous system's way of saying, *"I can't handle this yet help me hold it."*

When a child is upset, their body floods with energy: fast heart, shallow breath, tense muscles. If the adult responds with frustration or fear, the child's nervous system senses more danger. But if the adult stays steady breathing slowly, soft-voiced, grounded the child's body begins to mirror that state.

This isn't a trick. It's neuroscience. Humans are wired for connection. Our nervous systems constantly read one another's cues, facial expression, tone, movement, and rhythm to decide whether we're safe.

Co-regulation is that unspoken conversation happening beneath the words. It's what turns chaos into calm.

How the Nervous Systems "Talk"

When you hold a crying baby and sway gently, their breathing synchronizes with yours. That's co-regulation.

When a teacher lowers her voice and the classroom settles, that's co-regulation.

When you hug your anxious child and feel their heartbeat slow against yours, that's co-regulation too.

In these moments, your body acts as an external regulator, lending stability to theirs. Eventually, children internalize this rhythm learning how to calm themselves by recalling what it feels like to be safe with you.

That's how **self-regulation** is born not through lectures or punishments, but through repeated experiences of co-regulation.

The Cycle of Dysregulation

Many families fall into a loop of mutual dysregulation. The child screams, the adult tenses, voices rise, and everyone's nervous system goes into defense mode. Both sides are flooded; neither feels heard.

To break this cycle, someone has to become the calm anchor. And since the adult's brain is fully developed, that someone must be you.

This doesn't mean being perfectly patient. It means being **aware**. When you feel the urge to yell, pause. Take a breath long enough to notice your own heartbeat. Your body is your child's environment; the calmer it is, the more theirs can settle.

When adults model emotional recovery by taking a breath, softening their tone, reconnecting after conflict they show children that big feelings are survivable. That safety can return.

Repair: The Bridge Back to Safety

Even the most grounded adult loses their calm sometimes. What heals the rupture isn't perfection, it's **repair.**

After an outburst, kneel to your child's level. Make gentle eye contact. Say, "I got too upset earlier. I'm sorry if that felt scary. I'm calm now, and you're safe."

These words, delivered through a warm tone and steady gaze, teach something powerful: safety can be rebuilt. The body learns that connection is not fragile. This is what restores trust.

Repair doesn't erase what happened, but it rewires the memory replacing fear with relief.

Everyday Moments of Co-Regulation

Co-regulation doesn't just happen during meltdowns. It's built in the small, ordinary exchanges that fill a day.

- When you greet your child in the morning with a soft smile instead of a rush of instructions, you set their nervous system on a path of safety.

- When you notice restlessness at dinner and turn it into a game tapping forks or humming together you transform tension into rhythm.

- When a teenager retreats to their room and you quietly knock instead of demanding conversation, your restraint communicates respect and safety.

Connection grows in these micro-moments. Each one tells the child's body: *I see you, and I can stay steady with you.*

The Role of Rhythm and Play

Children regulate best through rhythm rocking, swinging, singing, drumming, walking in step. Rhythm is the nervous system's natural organizer. It creates predictability, a felt sense of "I know what comes next."

That's why lullabies calm babies and why even older children respond to patterned movement. Play, too, is regulation in disguise. Tag, dancing, building, coloring each helps the body discharge energy safely.

In somatic therapy, we use rhythm intentionally. A consistent beat, even in speech or breathing, gives the child's body a structure to rest against. It's the same principle that makes a heartbeat soothing in infancy, it says, *You're not alone in this rhythm.*

When Co-Regulation Feels Hard

Sometimes, a child's emotions are so intense that your own system gets flooded. You might feel helpless, angry, or scared. That's normal.

In those moments, grounding yourself is not avoidance, it's essential. Step back if needed. Inhale through your nose, exhale through your mouth. Feel your feet on the floor. Remind your body that you are safe. Only then can you become safety for the child.

If you notice your frustration rising again and again, that's information too. It may mean your nervous system is overextended. Rest, boundaries, and support are not luxuries, they're fuel for co-regulation. You cannot give what your body doesn't have.

A Story of Two Nervous Systems

During one session, I asked Ava's mother to try something different. The next time her daughter screamed, instead of insisting on quiet, she was to breathe slowly, audibly and say nothing.

The following week she reported, amazed, that it worked. "She still yelled," her mother said, "but then she looked at me and whispered, 'Are you mad?' When I said no, she just melted into my arms."

What changed? The mother's body stopped matching her child's chaos. She became a steady anchor instead of a second storm. Ava's body read that signal and responded: *It's safe to come back now.*

That's co-regulation in its purest form, the art of offering safety so the child can find their way home.

Practical Co-Regulation Tools

Here are simple ways to bring this practice into daily life:

1. Breathe First, Speak Second.
Before responding to a child's distress, take one full breath. Let your exhale be longer than your inhale. That's the signal of calm your body sends before your words ever do.

2. Match, Then Lead.
If a child is yelling, match their energy level briefly with a firm tone, grounded stance then gradually lower your volume. Their body will follow yours.

3. Use Touch Wisely.
A gentle hand on the shoulder, a hug, or even proximity can be powerful safety cues, but only if

the child welcomes them. Always ask or notice their comfort level.

4. Repair When Needed.

When disconnection happens, name it, own it, and reconnect. This teaches children that relationships survive tension.

5. Build Rhythms Into Routine.

Walking together, bedtime songs, or morning check-ins create predictable patterns the nervous system can rely on.

Each of these practices rewires both your body and the child's for safety. Over time, co-regulation becomes less of a technique and more of a way of being.

From Co-Regulation to Independence

The ultimate goal isn't for children to depend on adults forever, it's for them to internalize what safety feels like. When they've experienced enough moments of calm connection, their bodies begin to remember how to return there on their own.

A regulated adult creates regulated children. But the process also transforms the adult. As you practice staying present through another's storm, you'll notice your own nervous system becoming more flexible, less reactive, more compassionate.

This mutual healing is one of the quiet miracles of somatic work. In helping children feel safe, we rediscover our own safety too.

Reflection for the Reader

Think of a recent time when a child's emotions overwhelmed you.
How did your body react to tight shoulders, raised voice, racing heart?
What might have changed if you had taken one long, grounding breath before responding?

Tonight, try this: when your child becomes upset, say nothing for the first few seconds. Focus on your breath, your face, your posture. Imagine yourself as the steady anchor in a storm.

Watch what happens when your calm becomes their calm.

Chapter 4

Somatic Awareness: Teaching Kids to Notice Their Bodies

The Day Sophie Found Her Breath

Sophie was seven and quick to cry. Not because she was fragile, but because her body always seemed to overflow. When she felt angry, her face flushed. When embarrassed, she covered her ears. Her teacher called her "dramatic." Her parents called her "sensitive."

In one session, Sophie was upset because her drawing didn't look "right." Her fists balled, her breath quickened, and she began to tear the paper apart. Instead of stopping her, I quietly said, "Can you feel where your mad lives in your body?"

She paused. Her small hand went to her chest. "Right here," she whispered.

That single moment of noticing instead of reacting changed everything. For the first time, Sophie learned that her feelings weren't monsters to fight, but sensations she could name and explore.

This is the heart of **somatic awareness**: helping children notice what's happening inside their bodies so they can understand, and eventually regulate, their emotions.

Why Awareness Comes Before Control

Adults often want children to *control* their emotions to stop yelling, stop crying, and calm down. But true regulation can't happen until awareness does. You can't manage what you can't feel.

Somatic awareness teaches a child to pause and *notice* before acting: "My stomach feels tight," "My hands are hot," "My chest feels heavy." This noticing creates a gap between feeling and reaction. Inside that gap lives choice.

Children don't misbehave because they lack discipline, they react because their bodies move faster than their minds. Awareness slows everything down. It lets the child's brain catch up to the body's alarm system.

Over time, that awareness becomes second nature. A child who can say "I feel wobbly inside" is already halfway to calming down.

The Inner Map: How Children Learn the Language of Sensation

Every feeling begins as a physical sensation. The flutter of anxiety in the stomach, the warmth of pride in the chest, the heaviness of sadness behind the eyes these are the body's emotional vocabulary.

Children, however, don't automatically know how to read this map. They need gentle guidance to connect sensation with meaning.

Start small:

- "Where in your body do you feel that worry?"

- "What color would your sadness be?"

- "Is your anger fast or slow?"

When we ask questions like these, we help a child translate physical energy into awareness. The goal isn't to label emotions perfectly; it's to help them feel safe noticing.

Even young children can describe sensations when language feels playful. They might say their anxiety feels like "butterflies," or their joy like "sparkles." Those metaphors are accurate and deeply useful.

The Science of Interoception

At the core of somatic awareness lies a lesser-known sense called **interoception,** the body's ability to notice internal signals such as heartbeat, hunger, breath, or tension.

Interoception is how we know when we're thirsty, when we're scared, or when we need to rest. For children, especially those who've faced chronic stress or trauma, interoceptive awareness can become dulled. Their brains learn to tune out internal cues because the signals once felt overwhelming or unsafe.

Somatic practices reawaken this sense. When we help a child notice their breath, heartbeat, or muscle tension, we're actually strengthening neural pathways that connect the body's sensations to the thinking brain. That's the bridge between reaction and reflection.

The more children learn to identify sensations early, the less likely they are to be hijacked by them later.

Making Awareness Playful

Children learn through play, not pressure. Somatic awareness grows fastest when it feels like discovery, not discipline.

Try a few of these playful practices:

1. The Feeling Map
Draw an outline of a body. Ask your child to color where they feel certain emotions blue for sad, red for mad, yellow for happy. This visual exercise helps them associate sensations with meaning.

2. Weather Check
Ask, "What's the weather inside you right now?" They might say "stormy," "sunny," or "foggy." This creative language gives shape to inner states and invites conversation without judgment.

3. Animal Feelings

Invite them to name what animal they feel like a lion (angry), a turtle (scared), a butterfly (excited). The metaphor makes body states concrete and safe to explore.

4. The Breath Detective

Make a game of noticing breathing: "Let's see if we can find where your breath is hiding in your chest, your belly, or your throat."

Each exercise teaches noticing first, naming second. There's no wrong answer. The goal is curiosity, not correction.

Why Adults Must Model Awareness Too

A child can only notice safely what the adult can tolerate noticing. If we rush to fix or dismiss feelings ("You're fine," "Don't cry"), we teach them to mistrust their inner world.

Instead, model what awareness looks like:

"I notice my shoulders are tight. That tells me I'm getting stressed."

"I feel a lump in my throat. I think I'm sad."

When you speak this way, your child learns that sensations aren't shameful, they're information. They learn that paying attention isn't weakness; it's wisdom.

Your willingness to listen to your own body grants them permission to listen to theirs.

A Moment of Connection

Once, during a family session, I asked a father to place his hand on his chest and simply notice his breath. His son, who had spent most of the session hiding behind a chair, peeked out and copied him. Within seconds, the boy was sitting beside his father, both breathing slowly together.

No one spoke. The air softened.

That simple moment shared awareness did what hours of reasoning couldn't. The child's body recognized, *You're here. You're safe.*

Sometimes connection doesn't need dialogue; it only needs presence.

How Awareness Leads to Regulation

Somatic awareness is not an end in itself; it's the foundation for regulation. Once a child can notice their body, they can begin to experiment with what helps it feel better.

For example:

- "When I feel my heart race, blowing bubbles makes it slow down."

- "When my stomach feels tight, hugging my pillow helps."

- "When my body feels sleepy, stretching wakes it up."

The child begins to associate cause and effect with *my body, sends messages, and I can respond.* This sense of agency is profoundly healing for children who've felt powerless.

Awareness turns the body from something that "acts out" into something that *communicates.*

Helping Children Notice Early

The earlier a child notices tension, the easier it is to regulate. Waiting until a meltdown is like trying to stop a storm that's already raging.

Encourage children to check in with their bodies several times a day. You can make it part of routine:

- "Let's do a body scan before bedtime."

- "How does your tummy feel before school?"

- "Do you feel more like a balloon (light) or a rock (heavy) right now?"

These gentle check-ins teach children to notice the small signals before they turn into big ones.

Building a Safe Inner World

Many children who've experienced fear or unpredictability learn to disconnect from their bodies. For them, noticing sensations can feel unsafe at first. That's why somatic awareness must always happen within the context of safety and choice.

Never force a child to close their eyes, breathe deeply, or "relax." Let them decide how much they want to notice. If they say, "I don't feel anything," that's okay. Awareness begins with permission, not pressure.

Over time, the goal is for the child to feel at home in their own body not trapped in it. When they learn that sensations can come and go, they realize they are not their feelings; they are the observer of them.

That's emotional freedom.

Sophie's Discovery

A few weeks after Sophie's "mad in her chest" moment, we created a game called "Inside Explorer." Each session, she picked one body part and described what it felt like. Some days, her heart felt "bouncy." Other days, her stomach felt "squishy."

By the end of the month, she no longer ripped her drawings when frustrated. Instead, she'd take a breath and say, "My chest is starting to buzz." Then she'd squeeze her stress ball or stomp her feet with physical signals that helped her release the energy safely.

Her parents were amazed. The outbursts had softened not because she was told to behave, but because she had learned to listen.

When a child learns to feel without fear, they begin to live without chaos.

Reflection for the Reader

Take a few minutes to check in with your own body right now. Notice your breath, your shoulders, your jaw. What sensations present warmth, tension, tingling, heaviness?

Now imagine teaching a child to do the same.
How might your family or classroom change if everyone practiced this kind of noticing before reacting?

Tonight, try this:

Ask your child, "What does your body feel like right now?"

Then listen not to correct, but to understand.

That small act of attention might be the beginning of their lifelong safety.

Chapter 5

Movement as Medicine

When Stillness Feels Impossible

Eli was a bright, energetic six-year-old who couldn't sit still for more than thirty seconds. His teachers were frustrated; his parents were exhausted. During our first session, he spun in circles, knocked over a basket of blocks, and dove under the table.

When I asked him to take a deep breath, he froze, eyes wide. "I don't like quiet," he whispered.

That moment said everything. For Eli, stillness wasn't peaceful, it was unsafe. His body had learned that movement was the only way to keep the scary feelings away.

So instead of asking him to *stop* moving, I joined him. We jumped together, ran in place, and rolled a therapy ball across the room. After ten minutes, he collapsed on the floor laughing and still.

His body had done what it needed to do: release. The stillness that followed wasn't forced; it was earned.

That's the essence of somatic therapy for children, understanding that movement isn't the problem. It's the medicine.

The Body's Natural Regulator

Movement is the language of the nervous system. When a child runs, twirls, stomps, or wiggles, they're not just burning energy they're regulating.

Every emotion carries physical energy. Anger wants to strike, fear wants to flee, sadness wants to fold inward. When children are told to "sit still" while their bodies are full of unprocessed emotion, that energy gets trapped. Over time, trapped energy becomes anxiety, tension, or outbursts.

In somatic therapy, we give that energy a safe path to move through.

- Jumping helps discharge fight-or-flight activation.

- Swinging or rocking restores rhythm and balance.

- Stretching and pressing into the floor help reconnect the child to their body.

Movement tells the nervous system: *You're safe enough to feel again.*

Why the Body Must Move Before It Can Learn

A dysregulated body cannot learn, no matter how well-intentioned the teaching. The brain's learning centers focus, memory, reasoning depend on a calm, oxygenated, moving body.

That's why movement-based classrooms often see fewer behavioral issues and better emotional regulation. When the body is allowed to move, the brain becomes available.

Imagine trying to reason with a child whose body feels like it's on fire. No amount of logic can reach them until that energy has somewhere to go.

Movement first, reflection second.
Release before reason.
That's the order the nervous system understands.

The Science Behind Movement and Emotion

The human body is designed for motion. Every step, breath, and stretch stimulates the vagus nerve, the main communicator between the body and the brain. When this nerve is activated through rhythmic movement, it sends a powerful signal of safety.

Research shows that rhythmic, repetitive movements like walking, dancing, or drumming help synchronize the left and right hemispheres of the brain. This integration allows emotions to process more fluidly.

In trauma recovery, movement completes what the body couldn't do in the moment of threat to run, reach, fight, or shake. For children, this can look like playful activities: jumping on a trampoline, crawling through a tunnel, or spinning in circles until laughter takes over.

Movement frees the body to finish its unfinished stories.

Turning Everyday Play Into Healing

You don't need a therapy room to use movement as medicine. It's already woven into daily life if we pay attention.

- **Morning Stretch Ritual:** Start the day with a short stretch together. Reach high, bend low, shake out the arms. It grounds the body and signals a fresh beginning.

- **Emotion-in-Motion Game:** When feelings run high, ask, "What does your mad/sad/scared look like?" Encourage the child to show it with their body stomp, curl up, roar, sway.

- **Movement Breaks:** Between homework or chores, dance to one song, walk outside, or stretch together. The goal isn't exercise; it's release.

- **End-of-Day Unwind:** Before bedtime, do slow, rhythmic motions rocking, gentle swings, or shoulder squeezes to help the body settle.

When adults participate, it reinforces connection. The message is clear: *We move together; we calm together.*

The Difference Between Hyperactivity and Overflow

Many parents mistake hyperactivity for misbehavior. But often, what looks like chaos is simply overflowing a body flooded with sensations that have nowhere to go.

Children who can't sit still, who fidget, spin, or tap, are often self-regulating in the only way they know. Their bodies are saying, *There's too much inside me.*

Instead of demanding stillness, offer safe movement outlets: a wobble stool, resistance bands, a jump rope, or even a five-minute "shake it out" break.

Over time, as their bodies learn to discharge energy safely, stillness emerges naturally not as submission, but as peace.

Rhythm: The Body's Reset Button

Rhythm is the nervous system's favorite form of regulation. Think of a heartbeat, rocking chair, drumbeat, or lullaby. These steady patterns tell the body: *You're home.*

You can bring rhythm into a child's world through simple, everyday acts: clapping games, walking in sync, tapping feet together, or drumming softly on the table.

For children who've experienced fear or instability, rhythm restores predictability. It's like giving the body a map back to calm.

In therapy, rhythmic exercises often lead to breakthroughs not because the child talks about their feelings, but because their body finally feels safe enough to.

When Movement Brings Up Emotion

Sometimes, as the body begins to move, old feelings surface tears, anger, laughter, or even confusion. This is not regression; it's release.

The adult's role is to witness without fear. If a child starts crying while stretching or dancing, simply say, "Your body remembered something big. You're safe now."

Never rush to stop the expression. The body knows how to complete what the mind avoids. That completion is where healing lives.

Afterward, grounding activities help bring the child back deep breathing, pressing hands into a wall, or wrapping in a soft blanket. The goal is not to stay in the emotion but to let it move through.

The Adult's Body Matters Too

Your own movement habits teach children how to relate to their bodies. When you stretch in the morning, dance in the kitchen, or take mindful walks, you model embodiment.

But when you rush, stiffen, or ignore your physical needs, children notice that too. They learn that the body is an inconvenience instead of an ally.

Try checking in with your own body throughout the day:

- Have I moved in the last hour?

- What part of my body feels tired or tense?

- Can I take one deep breath before speaking?

Your nervous system becomes the template for theirs. Move gently, and they will too.

A Case of Transformation: Eli's Stillness

Over several months, Eli's therapy sessions became a blend of wild play and quiet grounding. Some days we pretended to be animals roaring lions, galloping horses. Other days we built obstacle courses to crawl and climb.

Gradually, the frantic energy shifted. After each burst of movement, Eli began to pause and breathe without prompting. One day, after running laps across the room, he flopped onto the mat and said softly, "My body feels happy and tired."

That phrase *happy tired* captured the transformation. His body was no longer stuck in fight-or-flight; it had found release and rest.

By letting his body move, we had given his nervous system permission to settle.

Movement as Communication

A child's movement is often their truest form of self-expression. When we look closely, we can read the message beneath it.

A child who hides under the table might be seeking containment.
One who spins might be trying to reorient after sensory overload.
Another who jumps constantly might be grounding through impact.

Movement always means something. Instead of stopping it, try to understand it. Ask:

"What does your body need right now?"

"Does it want to move fast or slow?"

"Do you feel bigger or smaller inside?"

These questions validate the body's wisdom and give the child agency over their own regulation.

Reflection for the Reader

Take a moment to reflect on your own relationship with movement.

When you feel stressed or overwhelmed, what does your body want to do: pace, stretch, curl up, walk? Do you let it, or do you force stillness?

Now observe a child in your life for one day. Notice when their body moves most freely and when it shuts down.

What might change if you saw every fidget, stomp, or dance not as misbehavior, but as medicine?

Tonight, try this together: put on soft music, and let your bodies move however they want for one song. No rules. No corrections. Just motion. Notice how the air feels afterward quieter, softer, lighter.

That's the body healing itself, one rhythm at a time.

Chapter 6

Touch, Breath, and Grounding: Tools for Emotional Safety

The Day Emma Finally Exhaled

Emma was eight and anxious about everything, loud sounds, new people, even rainstorms. Her parents described her as "constantly on edge." She chewed her sleeves, flinched at sudden noises, and rarely sat still.

During our first session, she perched on the edge of the couch, eyes darting around the room. Her body never stopped moving, fingers twitching, legs bouncing. I didn't ask her to talk. I simply said, "Let's see if we can find your breath."

She frowned. "I don't like breathing. It feels weird."

That told me everything. For children like Emma, the breath, their most basic lifeline can feel unsafe. When anxiety lives in the body, stillness can feel like surrender. Our work together would be about helping her *feel* safety, not just talk about it.

By the end of that session, we weren't discussing fears or strategies. We were sitting on the floor, our hands pressed into a weighted pillow, exhaling together slowly. Her shoulders dropped. For the first time that day, she sighed a long, trembling release.

That sigh was her nervous system saying, *Finally, I'm home.*

Safety Is a Sensation, Not a Concept

Children can't think their way into safety; they must *feel* it in their bodies. Touch, breath, and grounding are the primary ways we communicate safety to the nervous system.

Words like "You're safe" mean little if the body still feels under threat. But when a child feels your warm hand, hears your slow breath, or feels the solidness of the floor beneath them, their body begins to believe it.

Safety doesn't start in the brain, it starts in the senses.

That's why somatic therapy works through physical experiences first. By using gentle touch, mindful breathing, and grounding techniques, we show the body that calm is possible. Once the body believes it, the mind follows.

The Science of Grounding

Grounding helps children reestablish connection with the present moment through their senses. When the nervous system is flooded, it loses track of *now*. The child's body acts as if an old threat is happening again.

Grounding brings them back to what's real: this breath, this touch, this floor.

The body has three main grounding anchors:

1. **The Breath** — It connects the body and the brain. A slow exhale tells the vagus nerve, *You're safe.*

2. **Touch and Pressure** — Gentle, consistent touch activates the parasympathetic system, calming the heart and lowering cortisol.

3. **Sensory Awareness** — Feeling textures, noticing smells, or focusing on balance helps reorient the brain to the present moment.

For children, grounding isn't an intellectual exercise. It's sensory, rhythmic, and physical often disguised as play.

The Healing Power of Touch

When used appropriately and safely, touch is one of the most powerful regulators for a child's nervous system. It's the first language we ever learn long before words.

A hand on the shoulder, a firm hug, a soft blanket around the body these gestures tell the nervous system, *You are not alone.*

In somatic therapy, we often use **containment touch** gentle pressure that helps the body feel defined and secure. For example, weighted blankets or hand compressions on the shoulders can help a child who feels scattered or anxious.

However, touch must always be consensual and sensitive to a child's comfort level. For children with trauma histories, touch can be triggering. Always offer choice: "Would you like a hand on your back, or should we just sit near each other?"

The power of touch lies not just in contact, but in consent. When a child chooses touch, they're reclaiming control over their body. That autonomy is healing in itself.

Breath: The Body's Reset Button

The breath is the most accessible tool for calming the nervous system but for many children, it's also the most misunderstood.

When we say, "Take a deep breath," we often mean "control yourself." Children hear it as a demand, not a comfort. True therapeutic breathing is different; it's about *releasing*, not performing.

In somatic work, we teach breath through experience:

- **Belly Balloon:** Have the child place their hands on their belly and imagine inflating a balloon as they inhale, then letting it gently deflate.

- **Blowing Bubbles:** Each bubble carries a piece of stress away. This engages the breath without making it feel forced.

- **Animal Breaths:** Dragon breath (big exhale), bunny breath (short sniffs), lion breath (roar and release). Play makes regulation safe.

The exhale is magic. When the breath lengthens and slows, the vagus nerve signals, *All is well.*

Grounding Through the Senses

Sensory grounding helps bring children back from overwhelm by focusing their attention on something tangible. It's the nervous system's way of anchoring to "here and now."

Some easy, playful grounding tools:

- **5–4–3–2–1 Game:** Name five things you see, four you can touch, three you hear, two you smell, one you taste.

- **Magic Feet:** Press feet into the floor and imagine roots growing into the ground. Feel the body's weight supported.

- **Weighted Objects:** Small beanbags, heavy pillows, or blankets provide proprioceptive input to the body's reminder of "I exist."

- **Texture Hunt:** Let the child find something soft, smooth, rough, or warm. This brings awareness out of panic and into curiosity.

Each of these practices gives the body what fear takes away: a sense of place.

Creating Grounding Rituals at Home

Grounding works best when it's built into daily rhythm, not reserved for crises. Rituals make safety predictable and predictability is what the nervous system craves most.

Try weaving small grounding moments into your day:

- Morning: stretch, press palms together, take one shared breath.

- Afternoon: hand a weighted toy or soft object to hold during homework.

- Evening: gentle foot rub or slow breathing before bed.

These consistent sensory cues teach the body that calm is a daily habit, not a rare event.

Over time, children internalize these patterns. When they face stress later, their bodies remember what safety feels like even before their minds do.

When Safety Feels Foreign

For some children, even gentle grounding can feel threatening. If their bodies associate stillness or touch with past danger, they may resist.

When that happens, honor the resistance. Start small. Maybe it's just noticing the soles of their feet or feeling their breath in one hand. Never force.

You might say, "Your body gets to decide what feels okay today."

That statement alone restores agency, a key part of healing.

Gradually, as trust builds, the child's window of tolerance widens. What once felt intolerable (a sigh, a soft touch, a still moment) begins to feel safe.

This slow unfolding is the real work of trauma-informed care.

A Story of Touch and Trust

Emma's sessions became a choreography of grounding, pressing hands into the wall, stomping together, wrapping in a soft weighted blanket, matching breaths.

One afternoon, during a thunderstorm, she instinctively covered her ears and curled up. Instead of speaking, I gently placed a small beanbag in her hands and pressed one against her back solid, steady, unhurried.

Her shoulders dropped. After a few minutes, she whispered, "The thunder is outside, right?"

"Yes," I said. "And we're inside."

She nodded and took a deep breath on her own. The storm outside hadn't changed. The storm inside her had.

That's the quiet power of grounding, it doesn't remove fear; it teaches the body it can survive it.

Why Grounding Works for Adults Too

Parents and caregivers often forget that their own nervous systems need grounding as much as their child's. A dysregulated adult can't co-regulate a child.

Before helping your child settle, take thirty seconds for yourself:

- Feel your feet on the floor.

- Take one slow breath out, longer than your inhale.

- Drop your shoulders and unclench your jaw.

That single pause can change the entire interaction. You become calm in the storm and your body becomes the child's template for safety.

When adults ground, children follow.

The Body's Language of Safety

Children don't remember every word we say, but their bodies remember how we made them *feel*.

When your touch is steady, your breath calm, and your body grounded, you're speaking to their nervous system in the language it understands best.

In that language, "I'm here" means safety.
 "I'm breathing" means peace.
 And "We're grounded" means home.

Reflection for the Reader

Think of a recent moment when a child was anxious or upset.
What did their body need most movement, breath, or grounding?
Now think of your own body during that moment. Was it tight, rushed, or still?

Tonight, try a simple grounding ritual together:
Sit on the floor, back-to-back. Close your eyes.
Take three slow breaths in sync, inhale through the nose, exhale softly through the mouth.
Feel the weight of your bodies pressing against the floor.
Say quietly: "We're here. We're safe."

Let the silence that follows do the healing.

Chapter 7

Emotional Literacy: Helping Children Name and Express Feelings

The Boy Who Could Only Say "Bad"

Leo was ten and already known at school for his temper. He didn't hit anyone, but when he got upset, he'd crumple papers, mutter under his breath, and shut down completely. When I asked him how he felt, he gave the same answer every time: "Bad."

One afternoon, after a rough day at school, he sat across from me, arms crossed. I handed him a stack of cards, each with a feeling word and a matching face. "Pick one that feels close to what's inside," I said.

He hesitated, flipping through them: angry, hurt, embarrassed, disappointed. Finally, he pointed to *disappointment*.

"That one," he said softly. "It's when my stomach feels twisty."

That moment when "bad" turned into *disappointment* was the start of something powerful. It wasn't just about vocabulary. It was about self-awareness.

When children learn to name their emotions, they begin to understand themselves. And when they understand themselves, their world becomes less frightening.

Why Naming Feelings Matters

Emotional literacy is the ability to recognize, name, and express emotions in healthy ways. It's one of the strongest predictors of emotional resilience, empathy, and relationship success.

For children, feelings can be overwhelming a flood of sensations without names. When adults rush to fix, dismiss, or label for them ("You're fine," "Don't be mad," "Say sorry"), we interrupt their natural learning process.

But when we help them name what's happening "You're frustrated because the tower fell," or "You're sad because your friend left" we give them language for their inner world.

The moment emotion is named, it becomes more manageable. Brain scans show that labeling a feeling reduces amygdala activation, the part of the brain responsible for fear and reactivity. In simple terms: **naming feelings helps calm the body.**

How the Body and Emotions Connect

Every emotion has a physical signature. Anger heats the chest, sadness weighs down the shoulders, fear tightens the stomach, and joy lightens the breath.

Helping children link emotion to sensation builds somatic awareness and vocabulary at once. Try simple prompts:

- "What happens in your body when you feel mad?"

- "Where does happiness live inside you?"

- "If your sadness had a color, what would it be?"

This sensory approach bypasses the intellect and speaks directly to the body where the feeling actually lives.

When children learn that emotions have shapes, textures, and rhythms, they stop being afraid of them. They realize that feelings aren't forever; they move, shift, and pass like weather.

Teaching Emotional Language Through Play

Children learn through movement, imagination, and repetition not lectures. Emotional literacy grows best when it's embedded in play.

Try these engaging, low-pressure methods:

1. Feelings Charades

Act out emotions (silly, scared, excited, proud) and have your child guess. Then switch roles. It builds recognition and empathy at once.

2. The Emotion Wheel

Draw a colorful wheel divided into feeling

categories. Have your child spin or point to one and describe a time they felt that way.

3. Storytime Reflection

During books or movies, pause to ask: "What do you think that character is feeling?" or "Where in their body do you think they feel it?"

4. Feelings Journal or Drawing

Encourage older kids to draw or write what they felt that day, no corrections, no censorship. Just an expression.

5. Feeling Sculptures

Use clay or blocks to "build" what anger or joy might look like. This externalizes emotion, making it less intimidating.

The goal isn't to force emotional talk, it's to make curiosity safe.

Creating an Emotion-Safe Environment

Children will only name feelings when they believe they won't be punished or dismissed for having them.

That means adults must become emotional translators, not judges. Instead of:

- "Stop crying."
  Say: "Those tears are telling us something feels big."

- "Don't be mad."
  Say: "It's okay to feel mad. Let's find what your body needs right now."

- "You're overreacting."
  Say: "Your body feels this really strongly. Let's breathe and see what it's trying to tell us."

Safety doesn't mean avoiding emotions, it means allowing them without fear.

When a child knows their feelings are welcome, even the hard ones, emotional honesty becomes their default.

From Naming to Expression

Once a child can name a feeling, the next step is expressing it in a healthy way. This is where movement, creativity, and voice come together.

- **For anger:** punching a pillow, tearing paper, stomping feet, or drawing "angry lines."

- **For sadness:** cuddling under a blanket, listening to calm music, crying, or drawing rain.

- **For fear:** slow breathing, wrapping in something soft, talking through the scary thought.

- **For joy:** dancing, laughing, singing, sharing.

Expression completes the emotion cycle. Without it, feelings linger as tension or anxiety. When children move emotion out through the body, they make room for calm to return.

Helping Children Find Words That Fit

Every child's emotional vocabulary grows differently. Some are verbal; others express through art, music, or movement. The key is to meet them where they are.

You can introduce feeling words gradually not in a lecture, but in context:

- "You look disappointed that we can't go to the park."

- "You seem proud of your project."

- "I notice your body looks tense. Are you worried?

Each of these small moments teaches emotional labeling *in real time*, when the body is feeling it. That's when learning sticks.

Modeling Emotional Honesty as Adults

Children learn most from what we model. When adults hide or deny emotions, children internalize the message that feelings are unsafe or shameful.

Model emotional honesty in everyday life:

"I feel frustrated right now, so I'm going to take a breath."

"I'm sad because my friend moved away."

"I'm really proud of myself for finishing that task."

When you name your own feelings calmly, children learn that emotions can coexist with control. They see that expressing doesn't mean losing composure, it means being real.

That's emotional maturity in action.

A Case of New Language: Leo's Voice

After several weeks, Leo's "bad" became a collection of words frustrated, worried, tired, left out.

One day, after an argument at home, he sat quietly and said, "I think my mad is really hurt wearing a costume."

That metaphor *hurt wearing a costume* was brilliant. He had discovered that anger was protecting something softer underneath. When I asked what might help the "hurt part," he said, "Maybe a hug. But not yet."

That's emotional literacy at work: awareness, honesty, and boundaries all born from naming.

The Role of the Body in Emotional Literacy

The body is both the messenger and the translator of emotion. A clenched jaw might say "I'm scared." A bouncing leg might say "I'm restless." A sigh might say "I'm safe again."

By pairing body awareness with emotional language, children build a full emotional intelligence one that's felt, not memorized.

Ask often:

"What does your body feel like right now?"

"What do you think that feeling wants you to know?"

This not only develops language, it teaches self-trust.

Reflection for the Reader

Think of the last time a child expressed a big emotion.

How did you respond with curiosity or correction? What might have changed if you had helped them name what they felt instead of judging it?

Tonight, try this:
At dinner or bedtime, ask, "What was one feeling you felt today?"
If they say "I don't know," offer your own: "I felt tired when I had too much to do."
Keep it brief, kind, and real.
Over time, these small conversations become the emotional vocabulary of your relationship.

Chapter 8

Play, Creativity, and Healing Through Imagination

The Castle That Built Safety

When six-year-old Nora came to therapy, she barely spoke. She hid behind her mother and avoided eye contact. But in our third session, she spotted a box of toy animals and blocks. Without saying a word, she began to build a castle with high walls and a single gate.

She placed a tiny lion inside. When I asked who lived there, she whispered, "The brave one."

Every week, the castle grew. Sometimes the lion fought off dragons. Sometimes it just sat and waited. Slowly, Nora began to speak for it first in whispers, then in full sentences. Through her play, her body and imagination found a way to tell the story her words couldn't carry.

This is the heart of somatic play therapy: the understanding that **play is not an escape from reality, it's the body's way of processing it.**

Why Play Heals

Play is how children make sense of their world. It's how they test ideas, process emotions, and experiment with control. In therapeutic settings, play becomes a bridge between the body and the mind, a language where movement, sound, and story meet.

When a child builds, draws, role-plays, or moves, their nervous system is doing real work: regulating, expressing, and re-patterning old memories. Through imagination, they can transform helplessness into agency, fear into mastery, chaos into story.

For example:

- A child who felt powerless might become a superhero.

- One who felt trapped might build escape tunnels.

- A shy child might use puppets to say what feels too big to say directly.

The imagination provides safety through metaphor. The child isn't talking *about* trauma; they're rewriting it symbolically and their body feels the difference.

The Neuroscience of Play

From a biological standpoint, play stimulates regulation and connection. When children play, their brains release oxytocin and dopamine chemicals that support trust, creativity, and learning.

Dr. Stuart Brown, a pioneer in play research, describes play as the "oxygen of human development." It integrates emotion and cognition, helping the brain form flexible pathways for problem-solving and empathy.

Rhythmic play, dancing, drumming, pretend sword-fighting activates the body's natural regulation system. It balances arousal and relaxation, teaching the nervous system to move between intensity and calm.

That's why play is not a reward for calm behavior, it *creates* calm behavior.

The Role of Creativity in Somatic Therapy

Creativity through art, movement, or storytelling gives shape to what words cannot. The act of creating turns inner chaos into something visible, tangible, and therefore manageable.

For children, creative expression bypasses the pressure of verbal explanation. A drawing, a song, or a made-up story becomes a safe container for emotional truth.

In somatic therapy, creativity serves three key purposes:

1. **Expression:** It lets the body release stored tension through action.

2. **Integration:** It connects sensory experience with meaning and story.

3. **Mastery:** It helps the child rewrite their narrative from victim to agent.

Every time a child moves, paints, builds, or plays freely, their body says, *I am allowed to exist fully.*

Imagination as a Safety Tool

Children who've experienced fear or unpredictability often use imagination to regain control. What adults sometimes dismiss as "fantasy" is actually an adaptive mechanism, a way to process life safely.

A child who invents invisible friends or magical powers isn't avoiding reality; they're rehearsing safety. In their inner world, they decide who's kind, who's strong, and what happens next.

Therapists can join this world respectfully not to correct it, but to understand it. When we ask, "What does your dragon protect you from?" or "What happens if the superhero gets tired?" We invite insight through metaphor.

Imagination allows healing to happen at a pace the child's nervous system can tolerate.

Somatic Play Techniques

Here are a few practical ways to use play and creativity to support body-based healing:

1. Movement Stories

Invite the child to act out stories using their body. "Let's move like waves," or "Let's show how a brave tree stands in the wind." This blends imagination with grounding.

2. Sensory Art

Provide clay, sand, water, or textured paints. The tactile sensations engage the sensory system, calming the body while allowing expression.

3. Puppet Conversations

Let the child speak through a puppet or toy. Often, deep emotions surface when they feel a layer of distance. "What does your bear want to say?" can reveal more than "What do you want to say?"

4. Safe Space Visualization

Ask, "If your body could be anywhere safe right now, what would it look like?" Then draw or build it together. The nervous system responds to imagined safety as if it were real.

5. Rhythm and Sound

Use drumming, humming, or tapping to regulate energy. Music and rhythm bypass the thinking brain and speak directly to the body's rhythm centers.

These activities don't need to be perfect or artistic. Their power lies in freedom and sensory engagement.

How Adults Can Support Healing Play

For many adults, play feels unfamiliar. We're conditioned to see it as childish or unproductive. But when you join a child's play world without trying to teach or fix you enter the space where trust is built.

Here's how to engage:

- **Follow, don't lead.** Let the child guide the story.

- **Stay curious.** Ask open questions: "Then what happens next?"

- **Mirror emotion.** If the child's play is intense, stay calm but engaged. Reflect feelings without judgment: "Your dragon looks really powerful today."

- **End gently.** When the play ends, help the child transition back: "Let's take a deep breath and say goodbye to the castle for now."

Joining play doesn't mean analyzing it. It means witnessing showing the child that their inner world is seen and safe.

When Play Gets Intense

Sometimes play reveals fear, anger, or violence. This can unsettle adults, but it's important to remember: **the child is not being violent, their body is remembering violence.**

If a child destroys towers or attacks toys, stay grounded. Offer containment through structure ("The toys stay on the mat") and reflection ("Your knight looks very strong today. What's he fighting for?").

These moments are not regressions, they're released. The body is completing an old survival pattern safely, in symbolic form.

Once the intensity passes, children often feel lighter, even joyful. Their nervous system has discharged energy that words alone could never reach.

The Healing Arc of Imagination

In somatic therapy, play follows a natural arc:

1. **Expression:** The child projects emotion outward through movement or story.

2. **Exploration:** They experiment with control, power, and roles.

3. **Integration:** The story softens, and new themes of safety and resolution appear.

Nora's "castle play" followed this arc exactly. At first, every session was about defending walls, guards, and battles. But as her nervous system settled, the castle gates opened. One day, she added a second animal, a lamb beside the lion. "They're friends now," she said.

The symbolism was unmistakable: safety had returned.

Through imagination, Nora's body rewrote its story from fear to connection.

Why Adults Need Imagination Too

Healing through play doesn't stop with children. Adults who reconnect with creativity through art, gardening, dance, or storytelling reawaken their own regulation systems.

When you create, your body reenters flow: breath deepens, muscles soften, time loosens. You're not escaping stress; you're metabolizing it.

Children sense this shift immediately. A playful adult becomes a safe adult, someone who can hold big emotions without panic.

So when your child invites you into a world of dragons, castles, or make-believe, accept. It's not just pretending. It's therapy for both of you.

Reflection for the Reader

Think of a moment when your child invited you into their play, maybe a silly game, a drawing, or a made-up story. Did you join or hesitate?

Next time, try stepping in completely. Let them lead. Forget time and "purpose."

Notice how your own body feels lighter, more present, maybe even joyful.
That's not a coincidence. That's co-regulation through creativity.

In play, we don't just help children heal.
We remember how to be whole ourselves.

Chapter 9

The Role of Parents and Caregivers: Becoming the Child's Safe Base

The Anchor in the Storm

When nine-year-old Mason began therapy, his mother worried he was "too emotional." He cried over small things, panicked when plans changed, and often clung to her at school drop-off. During our first session, he drew a picture of himself standing on a small island while waves crashed all around.

When I asked who could help him in the picture, he drew a boat with his mom inside. "She can come get me," he said. "But sometimes she sails away."

It was an innocent sentence, but it revealed everything: Mason didn't need his mother to *fix* the waves he just needed to know she'd come back.

That's what being a safe base means. Not protecting a child from every storm, but teaching their body that someone will always return.

Why Parents Are the Real Therapists

Somatic therapy may happen in a clinic, but healing continues or stalls at home. A child spends one hour a week with a therapist and hundreds with their caregivers. The adult's nervous system becomes the environment where regulation either grows or collapses.

Children don't learn calm through instructions; they absorb it through presence. When a parent is steady, breathing, and grounded, the child's body mirrors that safety.

This is why parents are not just helpers, they're co-regulators. They are the *therapy between sessions.*

A therapist can guide, but only a caregiver can offer the daily rhythm, attunement, and warmth that turn safety into a living experience.

The Science of Connection

Attachment research shows that secure relationships regulate the nervous system. When a caregiver consistently responds with calm and empathy, a child's stress hormones decrease and their vagus nerve the body's "safety switch" activates.

In somatic terms, the child's body learns: *I can come back to calm because someone helps me get there.*

This sense of security isn't built through perfection. It's built through repetition of hundreds of small moments where the caregiver notices distress, stays present, and repairs disconnection.

Every "It's okay, I'm here," every calm breath beside a crying child, every gentle hug after conflict rewires the body toward trust.

The Power of Attunement

Attunement is the skill of noticing and responding to a child's emotional and physical cues with sensitivity. It's less about *doing* and more about *noticing*.

It sounds like this:

- "Your voice sounds small are you feeling worried?"

- "Your shoulders look tense; let's take a breath together."

- "I see you're frustrated. I'm here when you're ready."

Attunement tells the child, *You matter. I see you, even when you're hard to see.*

When adults misread or overlook these signals, the child's body learns that expressing emotion is unsafe. But when we meet their cues accurately not perfectly, but enough of the time the nervous system relaxes.

Repair: The Secret Ingredient of Connection

No parent stays calm all the time. We yell, withdraw, or misread situations. But rupture is not the problem *disconnection without repair* is.

Repair means returning to the child after conflict and restoring safety. It might sound like:

- "I got too angry earlier. That wasn't your fault."

- "I see that my loud voice scared you. I'm calm now."

- "We both got upset. Let's try again."

This isn't weakness; it's modeling emotional recovery. Children who experience consistent repair learn that relationships can survive tension, a lesson that builds lifelong resilience.

In fact, repair moments are some of the most powerful regulators a nervous system can experience. They transform fear into trust.

Becoming the Body of Safety

Children don't listen to words when they're overwhelmed; they listen to bodies.

Your posture, tone, and breathing communicate safety more than logic ever will.

Here's what a "body of safety" looks like:

- **Voice:** Soft, slow, steady. Avoid shouting across rooms. Speak from calm, not command.

- **Face:** Relaxed eyes and gentle expression. The human face is a child's first mirror. Let yours say, *You're okay.*

- **Body:** Grounded stance, slow movements. Quick gestures or pacing signal danger to the nervous system.

- **Breath:** Longer exhale than inhale. Children subconsciously match your rhythm.

In moments of chaos, becoming physically grounded is the most loving thing you can do. You don't need the perfect words, your regulated body *is* the message.

Boundaries as Safety, Not Control

A safe base isn't just warm; it's firm. Boundaries are the structure that tells a child, "You're safe, and I'm in charge of keeping it that way."

Many caregivers mistake somatic compassion for permissiveness, but safety thrives on predictability.
 You can be both kind and firm, calm in tone, clear in direction.

For example:

- Instead of "Stop that right now!" try "I won't let you throw that, it's not safe. Let's find another way to get the energy out."

- Instead of "Because I said so," try "My job is to keep us safe, and right now that means…"

When limits are set from calm authority rather than fear, the child's body relaxes into trust. Boundaries are love made visible.

Caring for Your Own Nervous System

Parenting a dysregulated child can be exhausting. You cannot co-regulate from an empty tank.
 Self-care isn't indulgence; it's responsibility.

Check in with your body daily:

- Do I need rest, movement, or stillness?

- Am I breathing fully, or holding my breath?

- Who supports *me* when I feel overwhelmed?

Children borrow regulation from adults but adults must borrow it from somewhere, too. Whether it's deep breathing, journaling, exercise, prayer, or therapy, find what helps your body return to calm.

Your nervous system is your greatest parenting tool.

Practical Ways to Be a Safe Base

You don't have to be a therapist to provide somatic safety. Small, consistent actions make the biggest difference:

- **Predictable Routines:** Consistency lowers anxiety. Keep mealtimes, bedtime, and transitions steady.

- **Physical Presence:** Sit nearby, offer gentle touch, or just stay close during distress.

- **Regulated Modeling:** When you make mistakes, show your recovery process aloud.

- **Shared Breath:** Take slow breaths together before hard moments "Let's take two calm breaths before we talk."

- **Naming Safety:** Say phrases like, "We're safe right now," or "You're allowed to feel that way." Repetition anchors the body.

Children don't need perfect parents. They need *predictable*, *present*, and *repairing* ones.

The Long Game of Regulation

Somatic safety isn't a quick fix, it's a relationship built over time. Some days you'll see progress, other days regression. The goal isn't constant calm, but a growing ability to return to it together.

Remember Mason's drawing of the island? Months later, he drew it again. This time, the waves were smaller, and the boat was closer. When I asked what changed, he said, "Now I know my mom comes back every time."

That's healing not the absence of storms, but the presence of trust.

Reflection for the Reader

Think about how your body feels when your child is upset.
Do you tense, rush, or try to fix it? Or can you stay steady long enough for their storm to pass?

Tonight, when conflict or chaos arises, take one breath before responding.

Feel your feet on the floor.
Remind yourself: "I am the anchor."

Because when a parent is grounded, a child learns the world can be safe even when it shakes.

Chapter 10

Integrating Somatic Practice at Home and School

The Bridge Between Therapy and Everyday Life

Nine-year-old Ava had made real progress in therapy. She could recognize when she was overwhelmed, use her breath to calm herself, and even guide her little brother through short grounding games. But her mother sighed during a session and said, "It all works here. The moment we get home, it's chaos again."

That sentence captures one of the most common challenges in somatic work with children: healing can't stay in the therapy room. To truly transform, these practices have to live where children live at home, in classrooms, on playgrounds, during family meals, and before bed.

Somatic therapy isn't a program to follow; it's a way of being with children. The real work begins when parents, teachers, and caregivers learn to weave body-based safety into ordinary life.

Why Integration Matters

A child's nervous system thrives on repetition and familiarity. One calm session a week can't compete with hours of daily stress or inconsistency. When somatic principles are practiced consistently in home and school environments, the body learns new defaults *calm instead of chaos, connection instead of withdrawal.*

Consistency is what turns coping skills into instincts. When a child repeatedly experiences grounding, empathy, and predictability, their brain rewires around those sensations. Over time, the "old story" of stress or danger fades, replaced by the steady rhythm of safety.

Integration also empowers caregivers and educators. It shifts the dynamic from "therapist fixes the child" to "we build safety together." Everyone becomes part of the healing team.

Somatic Parenting at Home

Home is where a child's nervous system learns its rhythm. Everyday routines can become small but powerful somatic interventions.

1. Morning Grounding Rituals

Start the day by connecting to the body. This might be a stretch, a shared breath, or a few moments of quiet before rushing out the door.

Example: "Let's press our feet into the floor and take two slow breaths before we go."

2. The Regulation Corner

Instead of a "time-out" chair, create a *calm corner, a cozy* space with soft textures, sensory tools, and visuals like a feelings chart or breathing guide. This teaches children that regulation, not punishment, is the goal.

3. Co-Regulation Moments

When tension rises, resist the urge to instruct ("Calm down"). Instead, join their body state first — lower your posture, soften your tone, slow your breath.

You might say: "Let's breathe together," or "I'm here with you."

4. Family Grounding Games

Turn regulation into play.

- "Heavy Feet" (stomping together to feel grounded)

- "Bubble Breaths" (exhaling through a wand)

- "Freeze and Melt" (tighten and release muscles to relieve tension)

When play becomes part of regulation, the nervous system learns joy and calm can coexist.

5. Repair Rituals

After arguments or meltdowns, make repair visible.

- "I got too loud. Let's take a breath and try again."

- "We were both upset. I'm still here. You're safe."

  These words re-teach the body that connection can survive conflict.

The Role of Rhythm and Routine

Children's nervous systems regulate best when life has a steady, predictable rhythm. Uncertainty creates stress; rhythm creates safety.

Establish routines that have somatic grounding built in:

- Morning: breathing or stretching

- After school: snack, movement, quiet time

- Bedtime: slow breathing, soft music, brief body scan ("Can you feel your toes?")

It's not about rigid schedules, it's about emotional predictability. When children can sense what's coming next, their bodies relax, and learning and play naturally flourish.

Integrating Somatic Awareness in the Classroom

Teachers are often the front-line nervous system support for children. With simple awareness and tools, classrooms can become places of emotional safety and regulation.

1. Normalize Movement
Children's bodies are designed to move. Integrate short "reset breaks" throughout the day stretching, walking, shaking hands, or quiet breathing. These small pauses reduce reactivity and increase focus.

2. Create Sensory Spaces
Have a small area with soft lighting, fidget tools, or a weighted lap pad where a child can self-regulate quietly. This isn't punishment, it's emotional maintenance.

3. Use Body Language Intentionally
A teacher's voice, posture, and facial expression

can either soothe or startle. Soft eye contact, gentle gestures, and a calm tone communicate safety more effectively than commands.

4. Model Regulation

When teachers say, "I'm feeling overwhelmed, so I'm taking a slow breath," it normalizes emotional honesty. Children learn that feelings can be managed instead of feared.

5. Encourage Empathy and Emotional Language

Integrate emotion check-ins during the day: "Before we start, what's one feeling in your body right now?" This builds emotional literacy and group connection.

Schools that adopt trauma-informed, body-aware approaches often see fewer behavioral issues, stronger peer relationships, and higher engagement because regulated kids can learn.

Bridging Home and School Communication

Children feel safest when the adults in their lives speak the same emotional language. When caregivers and teachers collaborate, the child experiences a unified message: *You're supported everywhere you go.*

Ways to bridge communication:

- Share simple summaries of what helps the child regulate ("She does well when given space to breathe before transitions").

- Use shared vocabulary like "grounding time" or "calm space" so the child hears consistency across environments.

- Celebrate progress together. When a teacher notices a child using their coping tools, communicate that to parents. This reinforces self-trust in the child.

Healing becomes seamless when school and home align around body-based awareness.

Challenges in Integration and How to Handle Them

Sometimes, families or schools resist somatic practices because they seem abstract or time-consuming. Others may expect immediate results. It's important to remember: nervous systems change through safety and repetition, not pressure.

If a child resists grounding or breathing, don't force it. Offer a choice instead: "Would you like to stretch or take a sip of water?"

If a teacher worries about losing classroom control, start with 30-second micro-practices. Even one shared breath can shift the energy in a room.

And if parents feel discouraged, remind them: regulation isn't about never losing control, it's about coming back faster each time. Healing is cumulative, not linear.

The Ripple Effect of Regulated Adults

Children's nervous systems are deeply relational. The calm of one adult can regulate an entire household or classroom.

When parents and teachers care for their own bodies through rest, breath, and boundaries they create a ripple effect of safety.

A regulated adult says without words:
You don't have to be perfect to be safe here.

That single message can change a child's entire developmental trajectory.

Ava's Story: The Home Practice That Worked

Remember Ava, the girl whose progress "didn't stick" outside therapy?

Her mother began weaving short grounding rituals into their day two deep breaths before leaving for school, a calming playlist during dinner prep, and a nightly reflection: "What did your body need most today?"

After a few weeks, Ava no longer saved her tools for therapy. She began using them naturally: breathing before tests, stretching when tense, even reminding her brother to "shake it out" when he was angry.

Her mother didn't need to control the process just to embody it.

Ava's body learned through imitation, not instruction.

That's the essence of integration: when safety stops being a technique and becomes a way of life.

Reflection for the Reader

Look around your home or classroom. Where could you build small moments of body awareness?
A calm corner? A shared breath before meals? A stretch between lessons?

Choose one simple practice and make it a daily ritual for a week.
Notice how the energy shifts in you first, then in the children.

Because somatic therapy isn't something we do *to* kids, it's something we learn *with* them.

And when safety lives in the body, it travels everywhere they go.

Conclusion

Coming Home to the Body

Every child wants to feel safe, seen, and connected. Somatic therapy teaches us that this safety doesn't begin in the mind, it begins in the body. Through touch, movement, breath, and awareness, children learn that their bodies are not enemies to be controlled, but homes they can return to.

For parents, teachers, and therapists, the work is simple but profound: to become steady enough for children to borrow our calm until they find their own. Healing doesn't come from doing everything right; it comes from showing up again and again, breathing through the chaos, and trusting that even small moments of connection matter.

A regulated body becomes a bridge between fear and safety, between silence and expression, between isolation and belonging.

When we help a child listen to their body, we give them the greatest gift possible: the ability to feel, to trust, and to come home to themselves no matter where they are.

Manufactured by Amazon.ca
Acheson, AB